I SPY ST. PATRICK'S DAY

BOOK FOR KIDS AGES 2-5

This book belongs to

- -

- -

I SPY WITH MY LITTLE EYE
SOMETHING BEGINNING WITH....

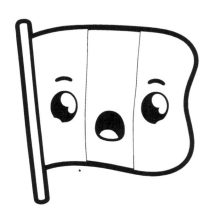

AIRCRAFT

I SPY WITH MY LITTLE EYE
SOMETHING BEGINNING WITH....

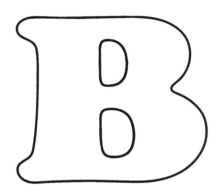

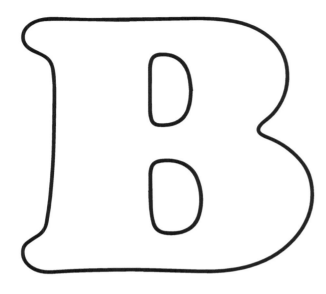

BOOT

I SPY WITH MY LITTLE EYE
SOMETHING BEGINNING WITH....

COINS

I SPY WITH MY LITTLE EYE
SOMETHING BEGINNING WITH....

D

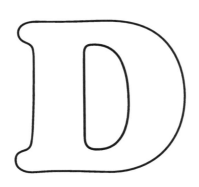

D

DUBLIN

I SPY WITH MY LITTLE EYE
SOMETHING BEGINNING WITH....

ELEPHANT

I SPY WITH MY LITTLE EYE
SOMETHING BEGINNING WITH....

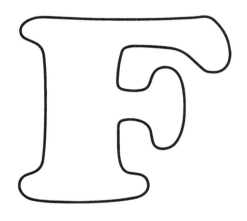

FALG OF IRELAND

I SPY WITH MY LITTLE EYE
SOMETHING BEGINNING WITH....

GOLD

I SPY WITH MY LITTLE EYE
SOMETHING BEGINNING WITH....

H

HAT

I SPY WITH MY LITTLE EYE
SOMETHING BEGINNING WITH....

IGUANA

I SPY WITH MY LITTLE EYE
SOMETHING BEGINNING WITH....

JELLYFISH

I SPY WITH MY LITTLE EYE
SOMETHING BEGINNING WITH....

KOALA

I SPY WITH MY LITTLE EYE
SOMETHING BEGINNING WITH....

LEPRECHAUN

I SPY WITH MY LITTLE EYE
SOMETHING BEGINNING WITH....

M

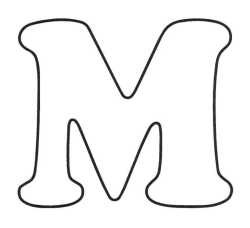

MAILBOX

I SPY WITH MY LITTLE EYE
SOMETHING BEGINNING WITH....

NARWHALE

I SPY WITH MY LITTLE EYE
SOMETHING BEGINNING WITH....

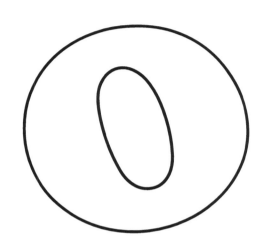

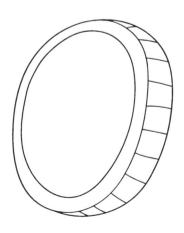

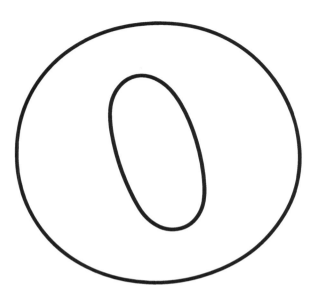

OWL

I SPY WITH MY LITTLE EYE
SOMETHING BEGINNING WITH....

P

P

POT OF GLOD

I SPY WITH MY LITTLE EYE
SOMETHING BEGINNING WITH....

QUEEN

I SPY WITH MY LITTLE EYE
SOMETHING BEGINNING WITH....

RAINBOW

I SPY WITH MY LITTLE EYE
SOMETHING BEGINNING WITH....

SHAMROCK

I SPY WITH MY LITTLE EYE
SOMETHING BEGINNING WITH....

TOP HAT

I SPY WITH MY LITTLE EYE
SOMETHING BEGINNING WITH....

UMBRELLA

I SPY WITH MY LITTLE EYE
SOMETHING BEGINNING WITH....

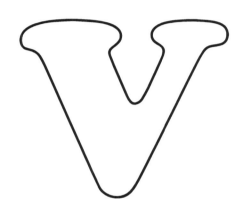

VALTURE

I SPY WITH MY LITTLE EYE
SOMETHING BEGINNING WITH....

WOLF

I SPY WITH MY LITTLE EYE
SOMETHING BEGINNING WITH....

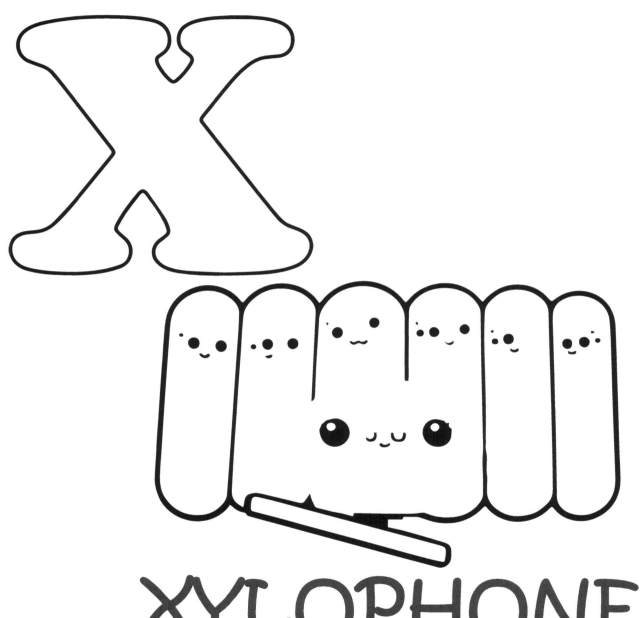

XYLOPHONE

I SPY WITH MY LITTLE EYE
SOMETHING BEGINNING WITH....

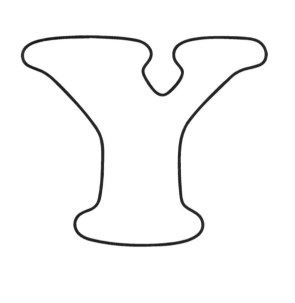

YAK

I SPY WITH MY LITTLE EYE
SOMETHING BEGINNING WITH....

Z

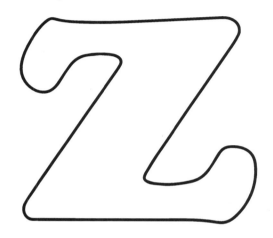

ZEBRA

Made in United States
Troutdale, OR
03/14/2024